Washington - Lee High School

AMAZING ICELAND

Photographs by Sigurgeir Sigurjónsson

Introduction by Helgi Guðmundsson

FASCINANTE ISLANDE

Photographies de Sigurgeir Sigurjónsson

Introduction de Helgi Guðmundsson

FASZINATION ISLAND

Fotografien von Sigurgeir Sigurjónsson

Vorwort von Helgi Guðmundsson

FORLAGIÐ

Amazing Iceland
Fascinante Islande
Faszination Island

© Ljósmyndir: Sigurgeir Sigurjónsson 1998
© Texti og ensk þýðing: Helgi Guðmundsson 1998
© Frönsk þýðing: Catherine Eyjólfsson 1998
© Þýsk þýðing: Helmut Lugmayr 1998

Umbrot: Ottó Ólafsson
Prentað í Singapúr
1. útgáfa 1998
2. prentun 1999

FORLAGIÐ · Reykjavík · 1999

ISBN Enska 9979-53-334-X
Franska 9979-53-335-8
Þýska 9979-53-336-6

Introduction

How is one to describe one's home country to people from abroad?

Should one tread the narrow path of strict objectivity or flaunt euphoric superlatives?

My approach is to deal mainly with matters unique to this country, things my own experience has taught me invariably catch the eye of travellers.

Iceland is a volcanic island on top of the submarine Mid-Atlantic Ridge stretching between the two poles. It is situated just below the Arctic Circle, where the adjacent North-American and Eurasian tectonic plates drift apart at the average rate of one inch a year. Consequently, a belt of active volcanism cuts across the central part of the country. It also follows that Iceland is geologically speaking very young and far from having reached its final shape. Magma from the bowels of the earth builds up on the surface to be counteracted by vigorous erosion by sea waves, rivers, glaciers and wind.

Earlier sources tell of offshore volcanism resulting in new islands that, nevertheless, have often been eroded down by the sea. The Westman Isles archipelago remains the most interesting in this respect, the youngest island, Surtsey, being just thirty years old and already considerably reduced in size by the combined effects of subsidence and ocean waves, providing a vivid example of the struggle between outer and inner terrestrial forces. The whole formative history of Iceland, indeed, may be considered an excellent textbook example of land formation and continental drift.

What still remains to be mentioned as an obvious formative factor is the lack of forests. Little is left of the birchwoods that originally covered a quarter of the land. The vegetation has been battered by 1100 years of settlement, to say nothing of volcanic ash and wind erosion. There are, however, many flourishing farming districts, largely subsisting on sheep and dairy farming.

A major part of the country is an uninhabitable highland plateau, and steep cliffs are very common along the coast. Glaciers cover approximately 10% of the total area, and lava fields a similar area. Apart from the south, the coast is indented by fjords. The major lowlands are to be found in the south; aside from these the remaining lowlands are restricted to narrow ribbons along the coast and valleys cutting into the highland plateau.

The climate of Iceland is cold temperate oceanic with cool summers and relatively mild winters, thanks to the Gulf Stream. Precipitation is considerable. There are numerous, mostly small lakes, and a multitude of streams, disrupted by innumerable waterfalls, flow to the sea. The largest rivers are glacial outflows, constituting some of the most fiendish natural obstacles that the inhabitants have had to tackle in their struggle for survival.

Iceland has always been geographically isolated, which accounts for the small range of animal life, except in the case of marine mammals, as there are hosts of seals and whales in the surrounding ocean. Bird species, however, are more numerous, and sea- and waterfowl, predictably, are dominant. Life conditions for seafowl are extremely favourable, with abundant food supply in the sea and excellent nesting habitats in the vast bird cliffs and thousands of skerries. Some of the bird populations are actually

3

among the largest known, for instance the Icelandic breeding stocks of Atlantic puffins and pink-footed geese. In fact the majority of these particular species breed in Iceland. Iceland is also an important stopover for arctic birds on their way between breeding areas north and north-west of Iceland and their wintering grounds further south on the planet. This applies especially to the western coast, that has the best feeding conditions.

Iceland is a harsh country, and natural resources like metals, coal and oil are nowhere to be found. Consequently the inhabitants have always been dependent on the import of necessities. In the past agriculture was the main livelihood, whereas nowadays fishery provides the basis of the economy. In this century, hydro- and geothermal energy has been harnessed increasingly, although these resources are still far from being fully exploited. These days most homes are heated by thermal spring water, thus saving enormous sums that otherwise would have to be spent on imported power-sources. These local power-sources cause very

little environmental pollution or damage, and remain among some of the most important pillars of the Icelandic economy.

The nation numbers a mere 270 thousand souls that are nevertheless capable of maintaining a modern industrialized society on this remote island in the high north. The standard of living is high, as are educational norms, and the Icelanders enjoy close relations with both their neighbouring continents on each side of the Atlantic. Technical knowhow is to an increasing extent being exported to faraway corners of the world, especially in the fields of ocean fishing and geothermal energy, where Icelanders, understandably, excel by virtue of homegrown experience.

Iceland was settled from Scandinavia during the Viking era, and to this day the descendants of the settlers speak their own language, Icelandic, which belongs to the West-Nordic branch of the Germanic languages. Due to isolation and stagnation in earlier centuries the language has been preserved relatively unchanged, virtually a living fossil

that constitutes the oldest living form of the ancient Viking tongue. Iceland boasts a strong literary tradition rooted in the dark ages, the medieval sagas being universally considered a unique contribution to world literature, for their time as well as today. Modern Icelanders are still able to read these ancient texts without much difficulty.

Thanks to its isolation and sparse population Iceland has remained relatively untouched. The majority of Icelanders now live in the capital area. The expansion of Reykjavík and other towns in this century has been at the expense of the rural districts, and this has led to the complete depopulation of some areas.

Iceland does not offer itself to mass tourism. Sunnier shores and easier living will always attract more visitors. Discerning newcomers will, however, soon discover some features peculiar to Iceland. Variety in scenery is great within a relatively limited area. Sparse population, clean air and lack of forests allow for great sightseeing, even within

the confines of a motor coach. Not to mention the fact that there are places within a 30-minute drive from downtown Reykjavík where one can experience the sensation of being "alone in the world". Indeed the purity of the air is such that visibility of, say, 80 miles is not uncommon. The same goes for the clear drinking water; in fact one can usually drink water directly from a stream.

What foreign travellers will probably value the most is nature itself, the spaciousness and the tranquillity. To be sure, gales may blow and rains may fall, so appropriate clothing should not be neglected, but most travellers have felt that these small inconveniences are outweighed by the attractions.

H.G.

Introduction

Celui qui veut faire connaître son pays natal à des étrangers n'a assurément pas la tâche facile. Il court le risque de se départir de l'impartialité sans faille qui est de rigueur et de s'abandonner à un discours dithyrambique. Comme toujours, le juste milieu est le plus difficile à trouver.

Personnellement, j'ai choisi de m'attacher à ce que je sais par expérience être susceptible d'éveiller la curiosité et de causer l'étonnement des touristes étrangers qui nous rendent visite - à ce qui constitue véritablement l'originalité de l'Islande.

La situation même du pays est l'une des premières choses qui viennent à l'esprit. L'Islande est une île au milieu de l'océan Atlantique, à mi-chemin entre le continent européen et l'Amérique du Nord. Cette île s'est formée sur l'une des lignes de séparation des plaques de l'écorce terrestre, au-dessous du cercle polaire arctique. Le pays fait partie de la grande dorsale qui s'étend du nord au sud au fond de l'Atlantique. C'est là que les continents s'écartent l'un de l'autre, de deux centimètres par an en moyenne, ouvrant le champ à une zone de volcanisme actif qui traverse toute l'Islande. Le pays est situé au-dessus de l'un des points chauds du globe, où le magma cherchant sans cesse à émerger des entrailles de la terre provoque de fréquentes éruptions. Il en découle que l'Islande, soumise à des changements constants, est en perpétuelle formation et est considérée comme une terre très jeune du point de vue géologique.

La force de frappe de la mer, les cours d'eau, les glaciers et les vents contribuent tous à la formation du pays. Des sources d'information de différentes époques font état d'éruptions sous-marines au large des côtes de l'Islande. Des îles et des pointes rocheuses ont parfois réussi à émerger malgré la puissance des vagues qui les rongent et les émiettent souvent au fur et à mesure. L'archipel des Vestman, au large de la côte sud de l'Islande, est très intéressant à cet égard. La plus récente de ses îles, Surtsey, vient de dépasser la trentaine. Elle s'est formée en majeure partie lors d'une éruption explosive dont les cendres se sont transformées en tuf, qui lui confère désormais un socle solide. Pourtant l'île s'est dégradée, sous les assauts de l'océan et les effets de son propre affaissement. Tout ici témoigne de l'œuvre des forces conjuguées de la nature qui s'exercent dans les profondeurs de la terre comme à sa surface. On peut dire qu'en Islande, l'histoire même de la formation du pays, pour ne pas dire celle de notre globe, saute aux yeux du spectateur.

Il est clair également que l'absence de forêts est l'un des éléments caractéristiques de l'aspect du pays. Au bout de onze siècles d'occupation humaine, il ne reste plus que les lambeaux épars des forêts de bouleaux qui couvraient, à ce que l'on pense, le quart du pays à l'époque de la colonisation. Et il en va de même, hélas, pour la végétation en général qui a beaucoup régressé, tant du fait des hommes que d'une nature hostile. Il a déjà été fait mention des éruptions ; il convient également de rappeler que l'Islande est la proie de tous les vents. Malgré tout cela, on y trouve des régions fertiles vouées à l'agriculture, notamment à la production de lait et à l'élevage des moutons.

La majeure partie de l'Islande est occupée par de hauts plateaux inhabités et les montagnes escarpées s'avancent souvent jusque dans la mer. Les glaciers recouvrent un dixième de la superficie du pays ; un autre dixième est enseveli sous les champs de lave des temps historiques. Les côtes sont très découpées, à l'exception de celle du sud. Les plaines, étendues surtout dans les parties sud et ouest, sont plutôt limitées par ailleurs et souvent réduites à une étroite bande côtière ainsi qu'à des vallées qui partent du fond des fjords pour se perdre dans les montagnes.

C'est un climat océanique tempéré-froid qui règne en Islande. Les étés y sont frais et les hivers relativement doux grâce au Gulf Stream. Les précipitations sont abondantes toute l'année. Les lacs sont nombreux, assez petits pour la plupart. Il en va de même des cours d'eau, dominés par les rivières glaciaires au courant puissant. La majorité d'entre elles, qui n'ont été enjambées de ponts qu'au cours de ce siècle, ont de tout temps constitué un obstacle aux communications et marqué la lutte pour la vie d'une population clairsemée dans un pays hostile.

l'Islande a toujours été isolée géographiquement parlant ; c'est pourquoi la vie animale n'y est pas très variée, si l'on excepte les nombreuses espèces de mammifères marins. Phoques et cétacés abondent tout autour du pays. Les oiseaux y sont nombreux, la plus grande variété régnant, comme on peut s'en douter, parmi les oiseaux de mer et les échassiers des marais. Les conditions de vie sont en effet particulièrement favorables aux oiseaux de mer, grâce à une nourriture abondante fournie par l'océan et aux lieux idéaux de nidification dans les immenses falaises et les nombreuses îles près des côtes. Certaines des colonies nichant en Islande sont d'ailleurs pami les plus grandes du monde, comme par exemple celles des macareux moines et celles des oies à bec court. Le pays constitue en outre une étape importante pour les oiseaux migrateurs du grand nord sur la route qui les mène de leurs nids du nord de l'Islande à leur lieux de villégiature hivernale situés sous des latitudes plus méridionales.

L'avifaune est particulière-

ment fournie sur les côtes ouest de l'Islande, où les grèves les plus étendues du pays offrent aux oiseaux les meilleures conditions pour se nourrir.

L'Islande a un sol plutôt ingrat, d'où les minéraux rentables tels que minerais, charbon ou pétrole sont totalement absents. Les habitants ont donc toujours été tributaires de l'importation de divers produits de première nécessité. À l'origine, les ressources principales de la nation provenaient de la culture et de l'élevage, qui ont été par la suite largement supplantés par la pêche. Ce n'est qu'au début de ce siècle que les Islandais commencèrent à exploiter la "houille blanche" des chutes d'eau et la chaleur des profondeurs de la terre. Ces sources d'énergie sont encore loin d'être pleinement utilisées. À présent, la plupart des Islandais sont chauffés par la géothermie, ce qui représente une économie considérable de devises. L'autre avantage de l'exploitation de cette énergie est qu'elle n'entraîne pratiquement aucune pollution de l'environnement.

Les Islandais ne sont que 270.000 et il est loin d'aller de soi pour une île aussi peu peuplée, située aux confins des terres habitées, d'être en mesure de bénéficier d'un état prospère où les conditions de vie de la population sont parmi les meilleures du monde. L'instruction publique est d'un niveau relativement élevé et les Islandais ont des contacts étroits avec les nations des deux côtés de l'Atlantique. Ils se distinguent par un haut degré de technologie dans les domaines de l'exploitation de la géothermie, de la pêche et du traitement du poisson. On s'emploie actuellement à faire de ce savoir-faire technologique une précieuse denrée d'exportation et les spécialistes islandais font de plus en plus profiter de leur expertise de lointaines parties du monde.

A l'origine, ce furent des vikings norrois qui s'établirent ici et leurs descendants n'ont cessé depuis lors de parler leur propre langue, l'islandais. Cette langue germanique, rameau du vieux norrois occidental, a subi relativement peu de changements du fait de l'isolement du pays et de l'évolution très lente de la société - au bord de la stagnation - au cours des siècles passés. Il en résulte que l'Islandais moyen peut encore lire aujourd'hui sa littérature médiévale sans grande difficulté. La littérature islandaise remonte au Moyen Âge et les sagas en sont incontestablement le fleuron. Ces sagas ont été un phénomène unique à l'époque où elles ont été couchées par écrit et elles sont encore aujourd'hui considérées comme l'apport le plus remarquable des Islandais à la littérature mondiale.

Du fait de son isolement et de la modicité de sa population, le pays est encore vierge à bien des égards. L'évolution des dernières décennies a conduit à un exode rural prononcé et plusieurs villages ont même été désertés pour toujours. La majorité de la population réside désormais à Reykjavik, la capitale, et dans les agglomérations limitrophes du sud-ouest du pays.

Il est douteux que l'Islande supplante jamais les plages ensoleillées du sud dans la faveur des touristes, mais l'environnement et la nature du pays ont un caractère à part et le paysage est exceptionellement varié. Dans un pays peu peuplé où l'air est toujours pur, la vue porte au loin et il n'y a pas d'arbres pour vous cacher la forêt. À faible distance de l'agitation de la capitale, on trouve des endroits tranquilles, propices à la solitude au sein de la nature. L'air peut être si transparent que la vue semble illimitée, et l'eau limpide des ruisseaux, ne nécessitant aucune purification, étanchera la soif du randonneur essoufflé.

Ce que les voyageurs étrangers apprécient sans doute le plus est la nature elle-même, l'espace et le calme. Le temps en Islande est cependant capable de jouer bien des tours et il vaut mieux être équipé de pied en cap pour affronter les intempéries. Mais cela n'arrêtera pas ceux qui veulent parcourir le pays et découvrir les beautés de sa nature.

H.G.

Vorwort

Wer die Absicht hat, anderen Nationen seine Heimat vorzustellen, steht zweifellos vor einer schwierigen Aufgabe. Es besteht die Gefahr, daß der Anspruch auf vollkommene Objektivität beiseite geschoben wird und dem pathetischen Ton einer Lobrede weicht. Der goldene Mittelweg ist - wie immer - schwer zu finden.

Ich für mein Teil habe beschlossen, mich auf das zu konzentrieren, was meiner eigenen Erfahrung nach das größte Interesse der ausländischen Besucher weckt - etwas, das man die Besonderheiten Islands nennen könnte.

Das erste, das einem in diesem Zusammenhang in den Sinn kommt, ist die Lage des Landes selbst. Island ist eine Insel im Atlantik, auf halbem Weg zwischen Europa und Nordamerika, an der Grenze zwischen den beiden Kontinenten am Rande des nördlichen Polarkreises ent-

standen. Das Land ist Teil des riesigen Gebirgsrückens, der sich am Meeresgrund von Nord nach Süd quer durch den ganzen Atlantik erstreckt, und an dem sich die beiden Kontinentalplatten voneinander wegbewegen. Die Kontinentaldrift beträgt im Durchschnitt 2 cm pro Jahr, und entlang ihres Dehnungsbereiches zieht sich eine aktive vulkanische Zone quer über Island. Unter der Insel befindet sich ein sogenannter "Hot Spot", an dem ständig Magma aus dem Erdinneren an die Oberfläche drängt und die Ursache für die häufigen vulkanischen Eruptionen darstellt. Island ist daher stetiger Veränderung unterworfen. Das Land wird ständig neu geschaffen und gilt in geologischer Hinsicht als sehr jung.

Die Erosionskraft des Meeres, der Flüsse, der Gletscher und des Windes tragen in weiterer Folge das ihrige zur Gestaltung des Landes bei. Zahlreiche historische Quellen berichten von submarinen Vulkanausbrüchen

vor den Küsten Islands.

Manchmal gelingt es Inseln und Felsklippen, sich über den Meeresspiegel zu erheben, und gegen die mächtige Brandung des Ozeans, der ständig am neugeschaffenen Land nagt, zu behaupten. Die Inselgruppe der Westmänner Inseln vor der Südküste des Landes ist in dieser Hinsicht besonders interessant. Die jüngste Insel der Gruppe, Surtsey, ist erst gut 30 Jahre alt und entstand zum größten Teil während einer heftigen explosiven Eruption. Mittlerweile hat sich die vulkanische Asche in Tuffgestein umgewandelt und der Insel Surtsey einen soliden Untergrund verliehen, obwohl die Brandung des Atlantiks und ein Absinken des Meeresbodens deutliche Spuren auf der Insel hinterlassen haben. Wir haben hier ein anschauliches Beispiel für das Zusammenspiel und die Schöpfungskraft der ungeheuren Kräfte, die im Inneren und an der Oberfläche der Erde wirken, vor uns. Man könnte sagen, daß

allen Besuchern Islands die Entstehungsgeschichte des Landes, und vielleicht ein Abriß der Erdgeschichte selbst, deutlich vor Augen geführt wird.

Etwas anderes, das das Erscheinungsbild des Landes auffallend prägt, ist das Fehlen von Wäldern. Nach der 1100 jährigen Besiedlung durch die Menschen findet man heute nur noch vereinzelte und ärmliche Reste der ehemaligen Birkenwälder, die zur Zeit der Landnahme etwa ein Viertel des Landes bedeckt haben sollen. Dasselbe gilt für die Vegetation Islands allgemein, die sehr unter dem Einfluß der Menschen und einer feindlichen Natur gelitten hat. Vulkanausbrüche wurden bereits erwähnt, aber auch das windige Klima spielt hier eine große Rolle. Trotzdem findet man an zahlreichen Stellen blühende Landstriche, wo Landwirtschaft, vorallem Schafzucht und Milchproduktion, betrieben wird.

Der größte Teil Islands wird von unbesiedelbarem Hochland eingenommen, und an vielen Stellen fallen die Küsten senkrecht ins Meer ab. Die Gletscher nehmen ein Zehntel der Landesfläche ein, und ein ebensogroßer Teil wird von historischen Lavafeldern bedeckt. Die Küstenlinie ist mit Ausnahme der Südküste stark durch Buchten und Fjorde gegliedert. Größere Ebenen findet man hauptsächlich im Südwestteil des Landes, während sich in den übrigen Landesteilen meist nur schmale Küstenstreifen und Täler befinden, die sich vom Meer aus weit ins Hochland hinaufziehen.

In Island herrscht kalttemperiertes ozeanisches Klima. Die Sommer sind kühl und die Winter aufgrund des Golfstromes relativ mild. Das ganze Jahr über werden nennenswerte Niederschläge verzeichnet. Binnenseen sind zahlreich vorhanden aber meist relativ klein. Dasselbe gilt für die Flußläufe, wobei die Gletscherflüsse die größten Wassermengen und Fließgeschwindigkeiten erreichen. Bis Anfang unseres Jahrhunderts

gab es so gut wie keine Brücken über die meisten der großen isländischen Flüsse, was ein bedeutendes Verkehrshindernis darstellte und großen Einfluß auf den Überlebenskampf des kleinen Volkes in einem harten Land hatte.

Die Fauna Islands ist wegen der isolierten geographischen Lage des Landes von einer Armut der Arten gekennzeichnet. Die Meeressäugetiere bilden darin allerdings eine Ausnahme, und man findet rund um die Insel Tausende von Robben und Walen. Ebenso kann Island als reich an Vögeln bezeichnet werden, wobei die größte Vielfalt an Arten wie zu erwarten unter den Meeres- und Wasservögeln zu finden ist. Das Land bietet mit seinem Fischreichtum im Meer und den zahlreichen Klippen und Inseln entlang der Küste ideale Brutplätze für Seevögel. So gehören etwa einige Populationen von isländischen Brutvögeln, wie z.B. Papageitaucher und Kurzschnabelgänse, zu den größten, die man kennt. Außerdem stellt die Insel einen wichtigen Rastplatz für arktische Zugvögel auf ihrem Weg zu den Brutgebieten nörd-

lich von Island bzw. zurück zu ihren südlichen Winterquartieren dar. Dies trifft vorallem für den Westteil des Landes zu, in dem sich die weitläufigsten Strände mit den besten Futterplätzen befinden.

Island ist eher arm an natürlichen Ressourcen, und Bodenschätze wie Erze, Kohle oder Öl sind nirgends zu finden. Die Einwohner waren deswegen seit jeher auf den Import verschiedener lebenswichtiger Grundstoffe angewiesen. Von Beginn der Besiedlung an war Landwirtschaft der wichtigste Erwerbszweig der Menschen, während heute die Wirtschaft des Landes zum allergrößten Teil auf Fischfang beruht. Erst zu Beginn unseres Jahrhunderts begannen die Isländer die Energie, die in den Flüssen und im Inneren der Erde steckt, zu nutzen, wobei die im Lande vorhandenen Reserven noch lange nicht ausgeschöpft sind. Der Großteil der Bevölkerung heizt heute seine Häuser mit natürlicher Erdwärme, was dem Volk eine Unmenge von Devisenausgaben erspart. Die Nutzung dieser Energiequelle hat darüberhin-

aus den unschätzbaren Vorteil, daß sie so gut wie keine Verschmutzung der Umwelt zur Folge hat.

Die Gesamtbevölkerung Islands beträgt nur etwa 270.000 Menschen. Es ist keineswegs selbstverständlich, daß eine so kleine Inselnation am nördlichen Rand der bewohnten Welt imstande ist, einen modernen Wohlfahrtsstaat aufrechtzuerhalten, dessen allgemeine Lebensbedingungen ohne Zweifel zu den besten der Welt gehören. Die allgemeine Schulbildung steht auf einem relativ hohen Niveau, und die Isländer pflegen gute Kontakte zu ihren Nachbarn auf beiden Seiten des Atlantiks. Sie überragen mit ihrer Kenntnis auf dem Gebiet der Nutzung von Geothermalenergie bzw. Fischfang und Fischverarbeitung heute die meisten anderen Nationen, und es gibt ständige Bemühungen, dieses Know-how zu exportieren. Isländische Spezialisten sind jetzt in zunehmendem Maße dabei, ihr Wissen in allen Teilen der Welt zu verbreiten.

Island wurde zu Beginn seiner Geschichte von nordischen Wikingern besiedelt, deren

Nachfahren bis zum heutigen Tag ihre eigene Sprache, das Isländische, sprechen. Isländisch gehört zur Familie der germanischen Sprachen, genauer gesagt zur Gruppe der west-nordischen Sprachen. Aufgrund der isolierten Lage des Landes und der langsamen Entwicklung im Laufe der vergangenen Jahrhunderte, die beinahe mit einer Stagnation zu vergleichen ist, hat sich die Sprache kaum verändert. Das hat zur Folge, daß die heutigen Isländer imstande sind, ihre mittelalterliche Dichtung ohne nennenswerte Schwierigkeiten zu lesen. Im Mittelalter liegen auch die Wurzeln der isländischen Literatur, deren bekannteste Werke ohne Zweifel die Isländersagas sind. Es gab zur Zeit ihrer Niederschrift kaum Vergleichbares in der mittelalterlichen Dichtkunst, und sie gelten bis heute als der bedeutenste Beitrag der Isländer zur Weltliteratur.

Wegen seiner isolierten Lage und der geringen Bevölkerungszahl ist Island in mancher Hinsicht ein unberührtes Land. Die Entwicklung der letzten Jahrzehnte hat einen Rückgang der Bevölkerung im ländlichen Raum bewirkt, und es gibt Beispiele dafür, daß ganze Landstriche entvölkert wurden. Heute wohnt die Mehrzahl der Bevölkerung in der Hauptstadt Reykjavík und deren nächster Umgebung im Südwestteil des Landes.

Island wird im Wettbewerb um mehr Tourismus wohl kaum jemals eine ernsthafte Konkurrenz für sonnige Südseestrände darstellen, aber die Natur und das Ambiente des Landes sind in vieler Hinsicht außergewöhnlich. Die Landschaft ist abwechslungsreich. Die klare Luft und die dünne Besiedlung bieten eine atemberaubende Fernsicht, die auch nicht durch Wälder behindert wird. Nur einen Katzensprung vom lebhaften Treiben der Hauptstadt entfernt kann man ruhige Plätze finden, die es einem erlauben, im Schoße der Natur mit sich allein zu sein. Die Luft ist manchmal so glasklar, daß man meint, die Sicht sei unbegrenzt. Dasselbe gilt für das Trinkwasser. Es muß nicht geklärt werden, und ein müder Wanderer kann in der Regel seinen Durst am nächstbesten Bach löschen.

Das, was die ausländischen Besucher wahrscheinlich am meisten schätzen, ist die Natur selbst, die Weite des Landes und die Ruhe. Das isländische Wetter kann allerdings manchmal rauh sein, und es ist ratsam, sich gut auszurüsten, wenn man dem Wettergott bei Wind und Regenschauer trotzen will. Diejenigen, die vorhaben, das Land zu bereisen und seine Natur selbst kennenzulernen, werden sich davon aber nicht abschrecken lassen.

H.G.

Inngangur

Þeir sem hyggjast kynna ættjörð sína framandi þjóðum eru óneitanlega í nokkrum vanda. Hætt er við að kröfum um fullkomna hlutlægni verði vikið til hliðar og hástemmd skrúðmælgi taki völdin. Líkt og endranær er meðalhófið vandratað.

Sjálfur hef ég valið þann kostinn að víkja einkum að því sem ég veit af eigin raun að vekur einlægt athygli og undrun erlendra ferðamanna sem hingað sækja – að því sem telja má sérkenni Íslands.

Sjálf lega landsins er meðal þess fyrsta sem í hugann kemur. Ísland er eyja í Atlantshafi, miðja vegu milli meginlanda Evrópu og Norður-Ameríku, mynduð á mótum jarðskorpufleka norður undir heimskautsbaug. Landið er hluti neðansjávarhryggjarins mikla sem liggur frá norðri til suðurs eftir endilöngu Atlantshafi. Hér rekur meginlöndin hvort frá öðru og á flekamótum liggur virkt gosbelti þvert yfir Ísland en landrekið nemur að jafnaði um tveimur sentímetrum á ári. Undir Íslandi er heitur reitur þar sem kvika úr iðrum jarðar leitar sífellt upp á yfirborðið og þess vegna eru eldgos alltíð. Af þessu leiðir að Ísland tekur stöðugum breytingum. Landið er sífellt að mótast og telst raunar mjög ungt í jarðfræðilegum skilningi.

Hafið með rofmætti sínum, að ógleymdum fallvötnum, jöklum og vindum, leggur einnig sitt af mörkum við mótun landsins. Heimildir frá ýmsum tímum greina frá neðansjávareldgosum undan ströndum Íslands. Eyjar og drangar hafa af og til náð að teygja sig upp úr hafinu þrátt fyrir öfluga úthafsöldu sem nagar af og brýtur oft jafnharðan niður aftur. Vestmannaeyjar, eyjaklasi við suðurströnd Íslands, eru afar athyglisverðar í þessu tilliti. Hin yngsta þeirra, Surtsey, er ekki nema rúmlega þriggja áratuga gömul. Eyjan er að mestu mynduð í þeytigosi en nú hefur gosaskan ummyndast í móberg og þannig hefur Surtsey öðlast alltraustan berggrunn. En þó hefur eyjan látið verulega á sjá undan ágangi úthafsins og einnig af völdum landsigs. Allt ber þetta vitni samspili og sköpunarmætti þeirra máttugu afla sem ríkja í iðrum jarðar og á yfirborði hennar. Segja má að myndunarsaga landsins, og í hnotskurn jafnvel jarðarinnar allrar, blasi við þeim sem lítur Ísland augum.

Einnig er augljóst að skógleysið er eitt af því sem ræður hvað mestu um ásýnd landsins. Eftir ellefu alda búsetu er nú aðeins að finna strjálar og fátæklegar leifar birkiskóganna sem munu hafa þakið um fjórðung landsins við landnám. Sama máli gegnir um gróður á Íslandi yfirleitt, að hann hefur látið mjög á sjá, bæði af manna völdum og óblíðrar náttúru. Áður var minnst á eldgos og þess ber einnig að geta að á Íslandi er ákaflega vindasamt. En þrátt fyrir þetta eru víða blómleg héruð þar sem menn leggja stund á landbúnað, einkum sauðfjárrækt og mjólkurframleiðslu.

Ísland er að langstærstum hluta óbyggilegt hálendi og víða ganga sæbrött fjöll í sjó fram. Jöklar þekja um einn tíunda hluta landsins og nútímahraun annað eins. Strendur eru mjög vogskornar ef suðurströndin er frátalin. Undirlendi er mest á Suðurlandi og vestanlands en er annars fremur takmarkað, yfirleitt er einungis mjó láglendisrönd með ströndinni og dalir sem ganga úr fjarðarbotnum upp í hálendið.

Á Íslandi er kaldtemprað úthafsloftslag. Sumrin eru svöl en vetur tiltölulega mildir vegna Golfstraumsins og úrkoma er töluverð allan ársins hring. Vötn eru fjölmörg en flest fremur smá. Um vatnsföll gegnir sama máli og eru jökulár mestar og straumharðastar. Íslensk stórfljót voru flest óbrúuð allt fram á þessa öld og hafa ávallt staðið samgöngum mjög fyrir þrifum og sett mark sitt á lífsbáráttu fámennrar þjóðar í harðbýlu landi.

Ísland hefur alltaf verið landfræðilega einangrað og af þeim sökum er dýralíf fábreytilegt ef frá eru taldar ýmsar tegundir sjávarspendýra. Allt umhverfis landið eru selir og hvalir í þúsundatali. Þá verður Ísland talið auðugt að fuglum og, eins og vænta má, er fjölbreytni tegunda mest meðal sjófugla og votlendisfugla. Lífsskilyrði sjófugla eru þeim afar hagstæð, gnótt fæðu í hafinu auk ákjósanlegra varpstaða í gríðarmiklum fuglabjörgum og ótal eyjum með ströndum fram. Reyndar eru nokkrir stofnar íslenskra varpfugla meðal þeirra stærstu sem þekkjast og má þar nefna bæði lunda og heiðagæs. Landið er auk þess mikilvægur áningarstaður hánorrænna varpfugla á farleið þeirra milli varpstaða norðan Íslands og vetrarheimkynna þeirra sunnar á hnettinum. Einkum á þetta við um vesturströnd Íslands, enda eru þar víðáttumestu fjörur landsins og langbest skilyrði til fæðuöflunar.

Ísland er fremur harðbýlt og verðmæt jarðefni á borð við ýmsa málma, kol eða olíu er hvergi að finna. Því hafa íbúar landsins ávallt verið háðir innflutningi ýmissa nauðþurfta. Í öndverðu var búskapur höfuðatvinnuvegur þjóðarinnar en nú byggir hún afkomu sína að langmestu leyti á

fiskveiðum. Það var ekki fyrr en við upphaf þessarar aldar að Íslendingar tóku að virkja fallorku vatnsfalla og hitann úr iðrum jarðar. Þessir innlendu orkugjafar eru þó enn langt frá því að vera fullnýttir. Nú orðið hita allflestir Íslendingar hús sín með jarðvarma og felst í því stórkostlegur gjaldeyrissparnaður. Að auki er það mikill kostur að nýting þessara orkulinda veldur lítilli sem engri mengun umhverfisins.

Íslendingar eru aðeins um 270 þúsund talsins og er engan veginn sjálfgefið að svo fámenn eyþjóð á norðurhjara veraldar skuli þess megnug að skapa sér nútímalegt velferðarríki þar sem lífskjör almennings eru óneitanlega með þeim bestu sem þekkjast. Almenn menntun stendur á tiltölulega háu stigi og landsmenn eiga náin samskipti við þjóðirnar beggja megin Atlantshafs. Íslendingar skara nú fram úr flestum þjóðum hvað varðar tækniþekkingu á sviði jarðvarmanýtingar og fiskveiða og -vinnslu. Er nú unnið að því jafnt og þétt að skapa verðmæta útflutningsgrein úr þessari tæknikunnáttu og íslenskir sérfræðingar miðla þekkingu sinni í auknum mæli til fjarlægra heimshluta.

Í öndverðu settust norrænir víkingar hér að og allt fram til þessa dags hafa afkomendur þeirra talað sína eigin tungu, íslensku. Íslenska er germanskt mál, nánar tiltekið telst hún til vestur-norrænna mála. Vegna einangrunar landsins og hægrar framþróunar samfélagsins á umliðnum öldum, svo jaðraði við nánast algjöra stöðnun, tók tungumálið tiltölulega litlum breytingum. Þar af leiðir að íslensk alþýða getur enn í dag lesið miðaldabókmenntir sínar án teljandi örðugleika. Íslenskar bókmenntir rekja upphaf sitt aftur til miðalda og munu Íslendingasögurnar án efa þekktastar. Þessar sögur áttu engan sinn líka þegar þær voru skráðar á miðöldum og eru enn þann dag í dag taldar merkasta framlag Íslendinga til heimsbókmenntanna.

Vegna einangrunar landsins og fámennis er það í ýmsu tilliti ósnortið. Þróun síðustu áratuga hefur leitt til þess að fólki hefur fækkað mjög á landsbyggðinni og dæmi eru um að heilu byggðarlögin hafi lagst af fyrir fullt og allt. Nú býr meirihluti þjóðarinnar í höfuðborginni, Reykjavík, og næsta nágrenni hennar á suðvestanverðu landinu.

Ísland mun varla nokkurn tíma geta keppt um hylli ferðamanna við suðrænar sólarstrendur en umhverfi og náttúrufar landsins er um margt sérstætt. Landslag er fjölbreytilegt. Í fámennu landi og tæru lofti er ákaflega víðsýnt og engir eru skógarnir til að byrgja mönnum sýn. Rétt innan seilingar frá ys og þys höfuðborgarinnar má finna kyrrláta staði þar sem má una einn með sjálfum sér í skauti náttúrunnar. Loftið getur verið svo tært að skyggni virðist nánast ótakmarkað. Sama er að segja um drykkjarvatnið, það þarfnast ekki hreinsunar og göngumóður ferðalangur getur yfirleitt svalað þorstanum við næsta læk.

Það sem erlendir ferðamenn kunna líklega best að meta er náttúran sjálf, víðáttan og kyrrðin. Íslensk veðrátta getur þó verið rysjótt og það er eins gott að vera vel búinn ef menn ætla að geta boðið veðurguðunum birginn í roki og rigningarhraglanda. En þeir sem vilja ferðast um landið og kynnast náttúru þess munu ekki setja það fyrir sig.

H.G.

AMAZING ICELAND
FASCINANTE ISLANDE
FASZINATION ISLAND

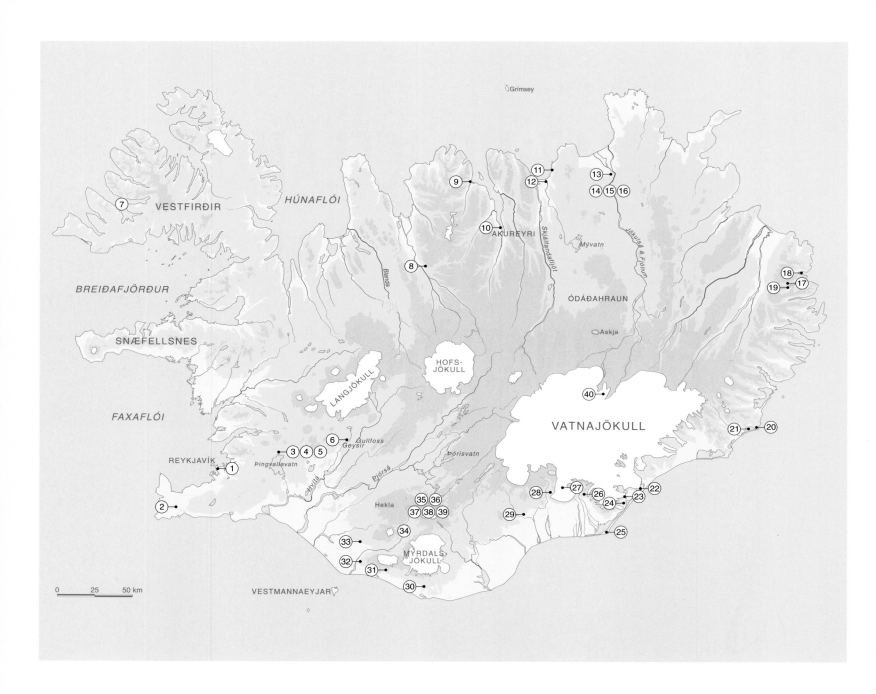

(1) REYKJAVÍK	(11) HÚSAVÍK	(21) LÓN	(31) EYJAFJÖLL
(2) BLÁA LÓNIÐ	(12) ÆÐARFOSSAR	(22) JÖKULSÁRLÓN	(32) SELJALANDSFOSS
(3) ÞINGVELLIR	(13) ÁSBYRGI	(23) FJALLSJÖKULL	(33) HLÍÐARENDI
(4) ÞINGVELLIR	(14) JÖKULSÁRGLJÚFUR	(24) KVÍSKER	(34) MARKARFLJÓT
(5) ÞINGVELLIR	(15) JÖKULSÁRGLJÚFUR	(25) INGÓLFSHÖFÐI	(35) LANDMANNALAUGAR
(6) STROKKUR	(16) JÖKULSÁRGLJÚFUR	(26) SKAFTAFELL	(36) LANDMANNALAUGAR
(7) ARNARFJÖRÐUR	(17) FOSS	(27) SKEIÐARÁRJÖKULL	(37) LANDMANNALAUGAR
(8) SILFRASTAÐIR	(18) LOÐMUNDARFJÖRÐUR	(28) NÚPSSTAÐARSKÓGUR	(38) LANDMANNALAUGAR
(9) DALVÍK	(19) SEYÐISFJÖRÐUR	(29) HVOLL Í FLJÓTSHVERFI	(39) LANDMANNALAUGAR
(10) AKUREYRI	(20) EYSTRAHORN	(30) MÝRDALUR	(40) KVERKFJÖLL

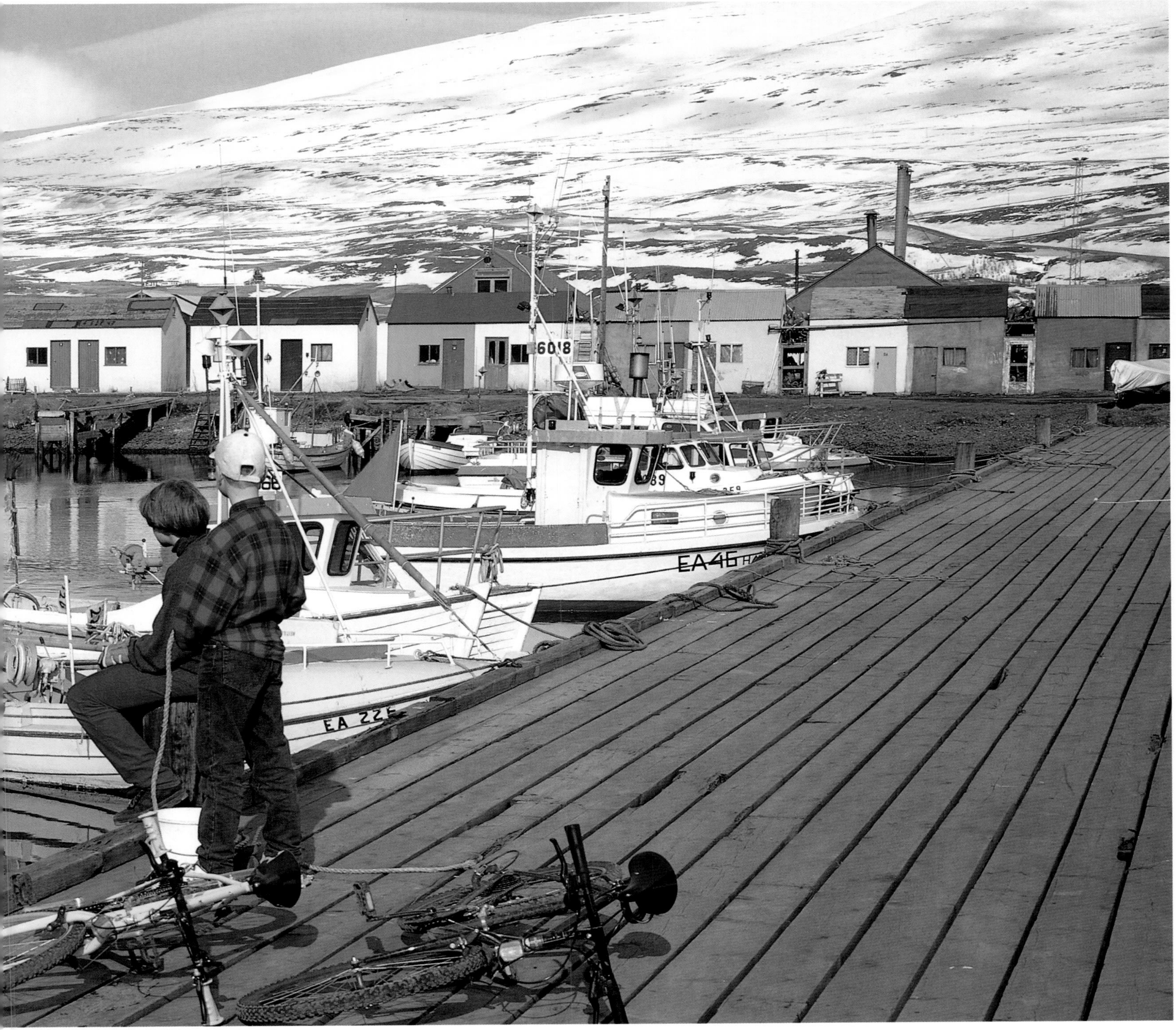
6018
EA46

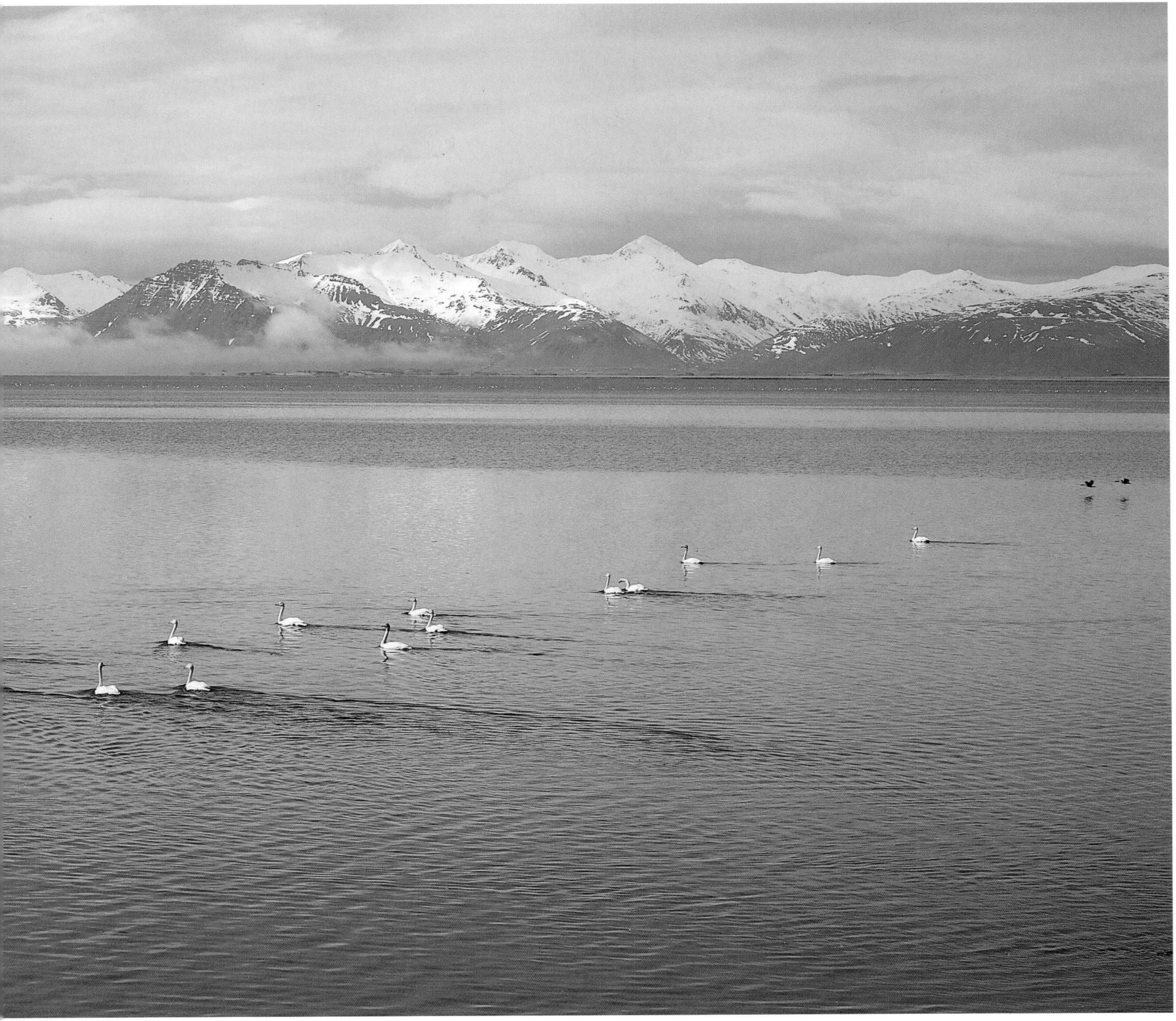

Washington-Lee High School